P9-EDN-259

The Bigger the Sign, the Worse the Garage Sale

The Bigger the Worse the

By Adair Lara Illustrations by Roxanna Bikadoroff

the Sign, Garage Sale

CHRONICLE BOOKS
SAN FRANCISCO

Library of Congress Cataloging-in-Publication Data available.

ISBN-10: 0-8118-5613-5
ISBN-13: 978-0-8118-5613-3

Manufactured in China.

Designed by Vivien Sung
Typeset in Super Grotesk and Grove Script

Distributed in Canada by Raincoast Books
9050 Shaughnessy Street
Vancouver, British Columbia V6P 6E5

10 9 8 7 6 5 4 3 2 1

Chronicle Books LLC
680 Second Street
San Francisco, California 94107
www.chroniclebooks.com

For Morgan, who has found that orange food rarely disappoints

Introduction

These are not the distillations of pundits, poets, and sages, but the rueful observations of ordinary citizens who have knocked around the planet long enough to learn a thing or two. Anyone who has tried to pass off a $29 Crock-Pot from Marshall's as a purchase from the gourmet appliance section of Macy's knows that those discount stickers require a blowtorch—and a little telltale orange is still left behind. My friend Donna is the one who keeps the number of her computer repairman in—you got it—her computer. People do care more about getting a bargain than they do about price. I know I'd rather buy a toaster for $2 at a garage sale than be given it for free.

This volume is a sequel to *Normal Is Just a Setting on the Dryer,* which began when my husband, Bill, and I were talking about Maria Shriver's book, *Ten Things I Wish I'd Known Before I Went Out into the Real World.* I asked friends and readers of my column in the *San Francisco Chronicle* what they had learned from being in the actual real world, as opposed to the Kennedy-cousin, married-to-Arnold-Schwarzenegger real world.

One woman said, "The garment must fit at the moment of purchase." I haven't gone into a department-store dressing room since without remembering that. As for the title, *The Bigger the Sign, the Worse the Garage Sale,* people who take the trouble to make an elaborate sign for their garage sale are taking the whole thing too seriously, and that will be revealed in the prices. Three bucks for a Masters of the Universe figure with an arm torn off? I think not. As someone wisely noted: "Not all experience reveals, but all revelation comes through experience."

Every woman
who gives herself
a new first name
used to be
called Cheryl

The **deli tuna salad** was not made today.

Sometimes **denial** is good.

We call it **pacing yourself.**

Orange food rarely disappoints.

You learn from your mistakes by making them,

One key to a happy life is to never,
under any circumstances,
Google yourself.

not by avoiding them.

You get a good job by proving you can handle a bad job.

When you're kayaking down a mountain stream with a friend,
shut up and listen to the *swish* of the paddles.

Cats are stupid.

Once you let one move into your house, you will not be rid of it until it dies a messy and expensive death of old age on the rug.

My father betrayed me.

He wasn't perfect.

The valentines that come straight from the heart are the ones that kids ten and under make for their moms, with those candy hearts glued on and tiny wet spots where ones fell off.

Don't sit on your towel and watch
your kid go down the water slide.

Go down with him.

Don't let your brother-in-law prepare your taxes.

Even though you know your recipe for turkey stuffing is *superior*, ask your mother-in-law how to make hers.

No matter how much room they take up, you can't throw away stuffed animals, because they have faces.

A cat makes a room look **peaceful.**

No one who cannot train a dog to

heel,

sit,

and stay

should be allowed to raise children.

You can be right all the time
or you can have friends.

The **leak** in the roof is **never** where the **drip is.**

The thing you **didn't notice** is the thing that **gets you** in the end.

Stick to your guns only if you know how to use them.

If they make you dig a trench, dig the most **gorgeous trench** anybody's ever dug.

No one will remember what you did or what you said.
But they will all remember how you made them feel.

When you are filling out that tax form or that self-appraisal for work, remember: people operate on the information you give them.

Just because you **can** doesn't mean you **should.**

Ruts are underrated. Ruts are what allow you to get good at something.

Your neighbor is making a racket and won't stop?

Inflate your *eight-foot Santa* and *snowman* and put them back on your front lawn.

Even if it's June.

Why shouldn't holidays be celebrated year-round?

Or take up the bagpipes.

Practice day and night.

What I learned from watching my
ten-year-old sweep the floor:

Patience is watching someone do something
you could do ten times faster.

How well you paint the inside of a closet is as good a measure of **your integrity** as anything.

Don't start thank-you notes with "thank you." Start them with something else and save "thank you" for later, and the note writes itself.

A good job can be a worse trap than a bad one.

You can never have too many white shirts.

Everybody ought to have one pair of **cowboy boots.**

Just for Men is perfect

for dyeing your eyebrows.

One box lasts forever.

To make a vacation especially blissful,
bring along work to ignore.

It's a lot easier to make people cry
than to make them laugh.

Only teenagers have the self-absorption and time, not to mention the coordination, it takes to learn to put on false eyelashes or get that perfect stroke with eyeliner.

By the time you get haggard enough to really benefit from makeup, you're too busy or too blind.

If you're over forty and haven't learned to put on your eyeliner, get it tattooed on.

If you wonder if your pants are too short, they are.

Don't ask yourself if you're happy.

Ask yourself *when* you're happy.

Take a few minutes every night to write down the times that day when you were most content.

The difference between *stress* and *stimulation* is your sense of **getting to choose.**

Don't boil eggs while writing.

It never hurts to ask: Beg the airline

attendant to bring you what they're pouring in first class.

"Smug marrieds," as Bridget Jones calls them, owe it to the universe to take enough time off from their domestic bliss to introduce their friends to each other.

Call your mother.

Go out in the sun. *It may not be good for you, but neither is cowering indoors, reading depressing tracts on the ozone, and dressing like a snowman to fetch the mail.*

Don't **pass up a chance** to smell a baby's head.

When in **doubt,** play by the **rules.**

Spend time with friends who make you **laugh.**

It isn't God but **humor** that allows us to
transcend our predicament.

Most things are on sale for a reason.

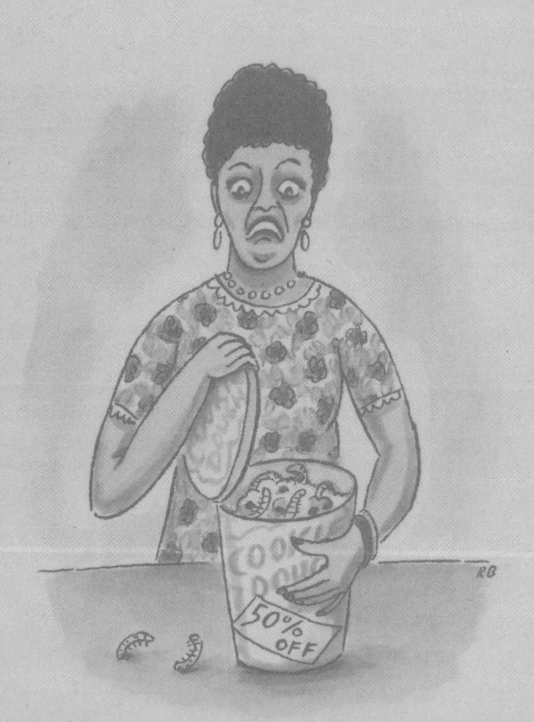

The price stickers at the **discount stores** are the hardest to get off.

Keep a catalog of gifts you intend to recycle (who sent each and when) so you don't get caught sending that tropical-fish lamp to anyone in the family of the person who gave it to you in the first place. If asked about an object's origins, say,

"I saw it on a wonderful little side street and immediately thought of you."

Ride the bus.

"Perfect hair" is a synonym for "Holy Grail."

Just because **you're not fat** doesn't mean
you can wear anything you want.

After giving birth, wear a girdle that's too big for a while.

Holds everything in!

Although the new Nair product looks like hair mousse, it is not. It is hair remover.

I have never regretted any trip I took, no matter how inconvenient, expensive, or unnecessary it seemed at the time.

I only regret the trips I didn't take.

No trip planned with friends after the third bottle of Pinot Noir will ever happen.

Or should happen.

Everybody in L.A. is from New York.

Order the chicken.

Get a *dog* so you'll always have someone who

No one looks good with a gray ponytail.

wags his tail at the mere sound of your voice.

Cheap thrill: Google an old flame.

If you have a drink before your ski lesson, having sticks on your feet and ice under you will feel natural.

Stop at one.

If you're not part of a couple, find someone to argue with you before you buy a vacation house in Scotland that's right next to the church whose bell tolls every quarter-hour.

No one looks good **chewing gum.**

When you find yourself laboring over your Christmas

letter as if it's *War and Peace,*

you know you're **a writer.**

Take your **unruly teenagers** out of town. As soon as you pass the county line, they will turn back into your children.

Everything of importance that I learned about my kids, I learned in the car.

A good enemy is worth more than any number of lukewarm friends.

Happiness:

Something to do, somebody to love, something to look forward to.

If you think it will improve your relationship with him or her, say it. Otherwise, don't.

You can trust a **handyman** who wears a **ponytail.**

When you hand kids a jar of crayons and some paper to color on at your antique mahogany table, make sure there are no Sharpies in the jar.

If God wanted us to ride motorcycles,
he would have made us headless.

Cooking aside,

"homemade" is a euphemism for "lovingly, dimwittedly screwed up."

Quit bellyaching and
go **help** somebody else.

A problem is as likely to be the stirrings of a new opportunity as it is to be the loss of a comfort.

Looking up at the sky will **cheer you up.**

Sometimes people don't want to be cheered up all the time.

Leave them alone.

Yes, you're scared, but go to the doctor anyway.

Almost everything turns out to be **nothing.**

It does matter **what you wear.**

When you go out to pick up the paper, smell

the morning air.

Sometimes talking makes everything worse. Go to a drive-in movie and hold hands.

Whatever you dream of doing someday,

do it now.

If you want to get to know someone, lend him money.

If you can say maybe, say *yes.*

Don't keep the number for your computer repairman in your computer.

Sometimes you **don't get credit** for things **you did.**

Other times you **get credit** for things **you didn't do.**

It evens out.

After a year of running,
I've learned it's all about
putting on my sneakers
and leaving the house.

Don't bring up the past.

If you're not making **anybody mad,**

you're not doing **your job.**

Emergency rooms are emptiest at 5 A.M. on Sunday morning.

Everybody uses the word *literally* wrong. Don't even try to use it. If you do, you will figuratively have egg on your face.

Reapply your lipstick.

Every piece of writing in which your mother appears is about your mother.

Be **nice** to your **friends.**

You never know when you are going to
need them to empty your bedpan.

Send your French fries back if they're not hot.

To say *"I'm trying"* is the sleaziest crutch of them all. Trying is a bid for credit for what you can't perform. Better to say,

"I'm going in that direction."

People using shoddy materials are rare. It's not that easy to find shoddy material—you have to go out of your way.

People care more about getting a **bargain**
than they do about **price.**

SALT
RB

Think **twice**

about someone who won't wear a costume to a costume party.

Make friends with the receptionist, the janitor, and your boss's assistant.

My choice for the **two best words** in the English language is

"summer afternoon."

When I was just *twenty-one* and out of college, I had an opportunity to go away on a special trip, sailing down the coast on one of those tall ships.

My father was adamant that I shouldn't leave my summer job—*how could I be so irresponsible?*—but my mother talked to my boss for me and drove me to the bus station.

She said she had many regrets about things she never did or never tried, and didn't want me to have the same kind of regrets. She used to say, *"Try it, just for ducks."*

Right turn on red is a sign of an enlightened polity.

Getting a **spot** on a brand new outfit is so

Take your meds.

dispiriting that it can be treated as not having happened at all.

If someone pronounces your name wrong, say, Lezzzlie instead of Leslie, correct them right away, so they don't have to think about how you've been seething for the past six months every time they passed your cubicle and said, "Morning, Lezzzlie."

You can tell a lot about a man by the way he handles three things:

a rainy day,

lost luggage,

and tangled Christmas tree lights.

If you're a mother, you can't say "Let's bounce." Remember when your own mom said "groovy"? No one wants a wannabe hip mom.

Make the preparation of every meal an **art project.**

Call him your **boyfriend** instead of **"my friend."**

"Boyfriend" conjures up leather jackets, convertibles, liquor in a flask, sex in the daytime.

When you are thinking about how much you like a friend, or admire him, call him and tell him exactly what you like about him.

If the doctor's office is full of Picassos, don't agree to cosmetic surgery.

After fifty, you have to fall back on **being yourself.**

It's your satisfaction that defines success.

Children who know what they want to be when they grow up are scary.

You're never going to start exercising at home, no matter how many home gyms or videos you buy, so just stop thinking you will. Homes are not about self-improvement. At home, you're already perfect.

Get back to painting.

Whoever you **love is your family.**

Could my health concerns be just a new way of hating my body?

Beware the open bar.

If your friend Lisa, whose long auburn hair always has the perfect amount of curl, shows you how to blow-dry your hair with a round brush, do not try it out the day of your job interview, unless you want to

(a) show up with a magenta boar bristle brush in your hair, or

(b) arrive at the interview five hours later with a one-sided mullet after an emergency visit to the hair salon.

Don't see any movie that's been called "charming."

Holding on to **resentment** is like eating rat poison and waiting for the rat to die.

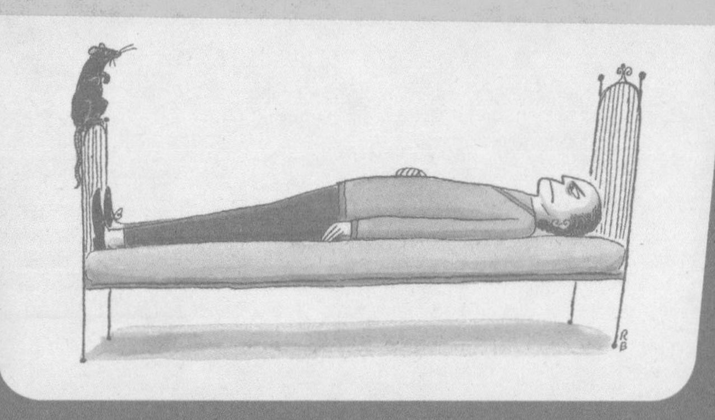

Forgive.

Even if your twelve-year-old daughter finishes off the Champagne and barfs in the potted palm, and you flub your lines and the cake melts and the band never shows but your wreck of a dad does, over your mother's dead body, and you spill orange juice on your dress and no one ever gets the coffee machine working, **the wedding was a success** if you stood up among a crowd of those you love and told the world you had something worth witnessing, worth celebrating.

A good marriage
improves with time,
like a good wine.

Getting fired

If you don't feel like cooking,

don't cook.

can be the **best thing** that ever happened to you.

Go out on the 31st of December, just out of morbid curiosity, to find out how awful it's going to be this time.

Everybody pretends to hate Christmas.

Then, when nobody's looking,

they race home and pull the curtains,
nail mistletoe above the doorways,
spray snowflakes all over the Venetian blinds,

and hang tinsel from the lamps.

A good dress is one that says your being the CEO doesn't mean that a tryst in the broom closet is out of the question.

Open your mail.

Having a say in your child's hairstyle is like trying to garden in your neighbor's yard:

it can be done, but you need very long arms.

Read the parenting books your children are **reading.**

Sulking is **silent whining.**

Give yourself permission to do nothing. Say to yourself,

"I will bob along in the current for six months, and if nothing has changed, then I'll do something."

Having a baby is the only legitimate way a married man can fall in love again.

Don't assume the grandchild's outfit is meant to be **ironic.**

The smaller the dog, the **bigger** the name.

If a person changes his or her hair, tell them *it looks good.*

Ask your interviewer,
"Do you think I **ought** to
take this job?" *(Gets them on your side.)*

Shop like a Marine. Buy a few good clothes.

Everybody's crazy.

No one's **life** was

ever changed by reading a little **book of sayings.**

If the color occurs in natural stone,
it will look good on your house.

The way to see beauty is out of the corner of your eye.
The only things worth seeing are those you all but missed.

Bullies respond well to *bullying.*

A good woman is superior to a good man every time.

Each of us is made up of three people:
the person we **think we are,**
the person **we really are,**
and the person **others think we are.**

Go to a drive-in movie.

Never make an **important decision** based on **one person's opinion.**

Always take the time to wait in line at a good restaurant.

Be nice, don't fight.

Sometimes it's okay not to have anything to say.

Extended warranties are for **suckers.**

If you don't know a word, look it up! Preferably in a dictionary that is fifty years older than you. That way, if the word is there, you will feel enlightened. If it's not there, then it's time to go out.

Gluing is hardly ever a good idea.

My mother said, **"You're as happy as you make up your mind to be."** It ticked me off when she said it, but now **I'm forty, and I see it's true.**

When later comes, my husband is going to be very busy.

Approach love and cooking with abandon.

Avoid radish chunks. Anyone who puts radish on a party buffet table knows nothing of the party spirit. In fact, if you see radishes, leave immediately. Go where they're serving chocolate-covered strawberries.

Do not have a snack before going to a party in an effort to control your eating.

The whole point of going to a party is to eat other people's food for **free.** Lots of it. *Hello?*

If my company was truly interested in treating everyone

equally, it would require all employees to wear bags on their heads.

If you are alone because someone left,

turn the radio to a station that particularly bugged that person and blast it. Pretend you are terribly sick and are therefore allowed to take the electric blanket and a hot toddy with lemon to the couch and watch *West Wing* back-to-back for three days. Remind yourself that you are no longer living with someone who can't leave a glass unwashed for five minutes, or who likes to turn on the heat and then open the windows to get a breeze.

If he hates it when you leave shoes by the back door, don't do it. You accept your mate after you accept that you can't change him or her.

The qualities that make your kids the spawn of the devil will make them **successful in later life**. The argumentative ones will be lawyers, and the one who stretched up high enough to put the cat in the freezer will be a basketball player and buy you a five-bedroom house.

Don't worry about getting that 1962 Buick running.

Sometimes the undone task, the potential achievement, has more value than the completed task:

it charges every idle, wasted minute with a strangely **compelling joy.**

Never have **business dealings** with anyone born and raised in **Oregon.**

Go to France,

even if France is just the spare bedroom with a picture of the Eiffel Tower in it.

Don't lose the ability to spend money, no matter how little you have. *Allow yourself the occasional small extravagance*—fresh flowers, a book not yet in paperback, the premium cable package.

When you want nothing from people, their powers end.

There are hardly any writers, outside of the federal penitentiary, who got started because they had time to kill.

You know how you **really feel** about someone when you get a letter from them.

Before you send your husband to the department store to buy that wonderful scent you found, make sure it's not room freshener.

Nude modeling is not a good way to get money to buy your family Christmas presents.

Fast money is not necessarily easy money.

Contributors

Deborah Frandsen, Laura Black, Maureen McVerry, Caitlin Flanagan, Joyce Renaker, John Flinn, Ray LeBlond, June Hudson, Eileen Halliburton, Anne Lamott, James Heig, Jamie Northway, Robyn Carr, Teresa R. Brown, Julia Lloyd, Lynn Befera, Ginny McReynolds, Robin Clements, John Jamison, Bill LeBlond, Gene Daly, Morgan Anderson, Nion McEvoy, Alyosha Zim, Carol Benet, Carol Costello, Annie Barrows, Monique Alonso, Georgia Zweber, Donna Levin.